How to Get Ahead in Work and Life

The "G" Element

**By
Tati So**

All rights reserved.

No part of this publication may be reproduced, stored in a retrieval system, or transmitted in any form or by any means—electronic, mechanical, photocopy, recording, or otherwise—without the prior written permission of the publisher, except in the case of brief quotations embodied in critical articles or reviews.

eBook ISBN: 978-1-967670-10-9
Paperback ISBN: 978-1-967670-06-2
Hardcover ISBN: 978-1-967670-07-9

Copyright Pre-Assigned Number: 2025907220
Publisher: Prime Publishing Studio

This is a work of nonfiction. Unless otherwise indicated, all the names, characters, businesses, places, events, and incidents in this book are either the product of the author's experience or used factually. Any resemblance to actual persons, living or dead, or actual events is purely coincidental.

Printed in the United States of America

Dedication

To my father God (YHWY, Yahshua) for being in my life and controlling my path, bringing all the wonderful people to bless me and taking away all the ones who did not fit our path. God, thank you for taking care of me all the days of my life and fulfilling all the promises we talked about and all my heart's desires.

To my mother, the most amazing mother, and the woman I love so much, thank you for loving me. To Robert C. Barnes, for being like the father I needed and never had. To my husband and daughter, for understanding and supporting me.

Tati So

About the Author

Brought over from South Korea with her mother as first-generation immigrants facing prejudice and poverty. My mother and I were abandoned by my biological father. Our Korean grandfather and oldest uncle exiled my mother and I from South Korea. Neither my mother nor I spoke a word of English when we arrived in the United States. Living in our first home with no running water or electricity. Life seemed bleak and filled with despair. At an early aged, I realized my mother was blessed. Understanding when you are more blessed than others oppression comes harder at you. Fighting the odds of poverty and prejudice God allowed my mother and family to be blessed. Always bringing blessings at the right time but right up the last-minute. I developed a personal covenant with God and understood my purpose as a teacher, developer, and how to overcome each dismal situation through faith and the empowerment from God.

Always striving to being a blessing to others. This book is my dedication to God to witness and bring others understanding, faith, and hope. Having individuals lean on God with understanding there is always a plan for you when you serve HIM.

I can remember God answering every prayer I prayed. I want this for you as my readers. Develop your relationship with God and allow HIM to show you and prove to you HE is always here for you.

Preface

Thank you for taking time out of your busy schedule to read this book. You may be looking for another avenue not yet explored to move you ahead in your job or you are here because you need something extremely specific to get you ahead in life. God (known as YHWH, Yahshua, Jesus) has brought you here. This encounter is not a coincidence.

This book is written in a context of Godly values, which can be taken and utilized for anyone needing clarity, understanding, or help. You have asked yourself a million times, "Why can I not get ahead?" There are things no one tells you. How do you get a competitive advantage? Do I have to play the political game? Should I play politics to get a promotion? Why can I not get caught up on bills? Am I going to be in this situation forever? The answer is "No." God controls our situation.

We will look at the prejudice that we all have experienced at one time or another, stereotypes of women, and distinct types of people who want to take your happiness and ability to move forward. You will be able to recognize these characters and know how to maneuver them. We will unlock the ability to empower yourself and people around you. Knowing these details will allow you to attain a distinct set of skills and abilities to get ahead, have peace, and prosper.

This book is written from my Christian's women point of view. However, these principles can apply to anyone looking to unlock their prosperity and purpose.

Contents

Dedication iii

About the Author iv

Preface vi

Chapter 1 Introduction... 1

Chapter 2 "The Struggle is Real" 2

Chapter 3 "Product of Your Environment"............................. 6

Chapter 4 "Let us Get into It"... 16

Chapter 5 "Characters We Have to Deal with on a Daily Basis" 27

Chapter 6 "The Right Mindset- The G Element" 38

Chapter 7 "The Principles of Sowing and Reaping" 42

Chapter 8 Perseverance and Endurance................................. 51

Chapter 9 "Role Model - Protecting your Reputation" 56

Chapter 10 "Why Is It Always Her?" 64

Chapter 11 "Expect Change." 80

Chapter 12 "Claim Your Purpose"... 84

Chapter 13 "Conclusion".. 90

Resources.. 94

Chapter 1
Introduction

This is not a fancy, scientific book or a book with all your perfect answers. This is not a long-drawn-out book. This book centers around only one thing understanding why we are in a scenario of why we cannot move ahead at different stages in life. How do we turn the tides in our favor to accomplish the things we desire and the things we need most? I am not a highly educated woman who has the secrets of the universe.

There is not a quick fix or a silver bullet to move you ahead like some books claim to do for you. You will have to work hard and be diligent every day. Some days will be easy, and other days will have you feeling depressed and oppressed. You will feel brow-beaten and defeated. Know this, I do understand the predicament you are in because I have lived it, I have been there where you are, I have seen the prejudice and stereotypes lived out in your life and mine.

I will share different scenarios you may be able to relate to or know someone who is going through the same scenarios. What you will find after reading this book is you are not subject to what everyone else is subject to. Right now, you may not understand this statement I made to you. By the conclusion of this book, you will understand "**You are not subject to what everyone else is subject to**" will be clear to you.

Chapter 2
"The Struggle is Real"

We all have heard of this phrase, "The struggle is real" or something very similar to this saying. Most of the time, we hear it or say it in a sarcastic tone or in a playful voice, but deep down inside, when you are all alone, we believe and live the struggle because it is REAL. What is the definition of the word struggle?

Struggle - Make forceful or violent efforts to get free of restraint or constriction.

How does God define struggle?

Struggle - forcible effort to obtain an object or to avoid an evil, violent effort with contortions of the body.

You may be working one, two, or three jobs to make ends meet. You may be going to school and taking care of young children, hoping to make a better life for yourself as a single mother. You may have to tend to a loved one because they are sick. When your day ends, you still must cook dinner, wash clothes and or clean your home. Have you ever had a child tell you right before bed they are out of school supplies or need something because the project is due TOMORROW? Let me tell you, my daughter is the queen of this scenario.

Your day begins at 04:30 am. You must get the kids up, fix breakfast, and get the kids to parent drop offline at daycare, school, or work. You are busy running errands. Is your adventure... you are feeling like a hamster on the same wheel.... over and over. The working women, homemakers are in a "daily grind." It is called a grinder because it chews you up and spits you out. You drive to work, not paying attention to the details of the drive because you have only enough energy to drive. You get to work and the only thing you can think of is, "I cannot wait until I get home tonight and lay down in bed." You arrive at work staying busy so as not to have a lapse moment. If you have one minute to think, you become distracted, and your mind starts wondering. Honestly, wondering about nothing really. You have co-workers that get on your "last nerve" every day. Yep, we are going to discuss these types of co-workers and individuals in your life. We all normally believe we love our jobs, or we at least tolerate what we do to keep from going down in a rabbit hole of despair and depression. You wish you could get a different position or another job. But you are not ready to start over or you cannot work the hours for the new position. You may be wrapping up your day and you are finally thinking, "Thank God It is over."

In the silence of your night, we get a moment to breathe. A deep sigh or exhalation and for a split moment, you draw a blank; your mind goes blank as if you are in a daze. Simply glaring into space not realizing what just happened. SNAP, back to reality and it is another deep sigh. You feel a heavy weight on your chest. The light pressure sits in that you cannot see our touch, but you know as clearly as you know your name it is there. You can feel tears wanting to well up in your eyes, your nose turns a little red and there are a few sniffles.

The phrase that comes to mind is, "If I knew back then what I know now, I would _____.

What would you really do differently? REALLY? All of you are finishing the blank space with different actions. Well, finish the sentence.

One fact is surely true, we have all felt this way at some time in our life or you will feel the same way sometime in life. You may feel this way for a small moment in time or you may feel this way every single day. You think I want something better for my life or my family or both. You begin to think to yourself, can I continue to do this? Don't I deserve more in life? I am a good person. There are things no one tells you to move ahead. Everyone wants to say, "It will be ok." You say to yourself, "BE, OK? You think to yourself, "I don't know if it will be ok." You think, "I am just so tired, sick and tired." Some days you think, "I am just tired of everything."

Here is the truth. The struggle will always be going to be there. Every situation will not be better. Right, now you are thinking, "Well, dang, duuuuuh, I already knew that. I am living in a real struggle every day of my life." You have not told me anything I do not know with certainty in my heart, you deserve to have and be in a better situation. You can have all that your heart desires. You are not a product of your environment or a product of your current situation if you do not want to be. You are thinking, but I am …you do not know what I am going through. I may not know your exact situation, but I can tell you I have been close, if not right, in the same situation as you. I might have experienced situations worse than your situation. God will speak to you and tell you how to gain favor.

Zechariah 7:3-5: "Should I weep in the fifth month and fast as I have done for so many years? Say to all the people of the land and to the priests: When you fasted and mourned in the fifth and seventh months during those seventy years, did you really fast for me? This is referring to Truth in Action. Are you in strife because of you and your struggle to right for God? They were struggling for 70 years. God tells them how to get favor from Him.

Psalms 43: Vindicate me O God and plead my case against an ungodly nation. Oh, deliver me from the deceitful and unjust man! For YOU are the God of my strength; Why do you cast me off? Why do I go mourning because of the oppression of my enemy? Oh, send out YOUR light and YOUR truth! Let them lead me; let them bring me to YOUR holy hill and tabernacle. Then I will go to the alter of GOD, to GOD my exceeding joy; and on the harp I will praise YOU O' GOD, MY GOD.

Chapter 3
"Product of Your Environment"

You have all heard the saying, "Product of your environment or product of your situation." Truth - in some respects this a true statement. Who says you cannot change your environment or situation? You cannot do it alone. But you can surely change it. I am about to tell you a story.

I was born in Seoul, Korea. My mother is a beautiful South Korean woman. My biological father is Caucasian (Welsh and Scottish). My father served in the Army in Korea from 1967- the early 1970s. My mother and father fell in love. (The tension and situation in Asia were not good at this time. Remember what was going on during the 1960s and 1970s (Vietnam War). South Korea had already seen too many wars. Two Korean wars and now the United States taking providence in South Korea fighting North Korea.) Having a half-breed baby was not accepted in my mother's family. As a matter of fact, it was worse than death. My Korean grandfather and oldest Korean uncle gave my mother a few choices. My mother's choices were 1) **kill** the baby 2) **sell** the baby or 3**) throw the baby away** 4) **leave the country,** exiled from her family, leaving with nothing. (Which choice do you think you would have made?)

This was a terrible situation. My mother was a business woman owning her own home in Seoul. She had a nanny for me, cook, and handy man. My mother had done well for herself, considering she had been through two wars. We had a good life. My biological father abandoned my mother and me a few months before I was born. Here is where the tides turn. My mother recently became saved by God. My mother told me this story several times and even now tells me the story. She had a dream that God came to her and sat by her bed one evening in her dream. God tells my mother not to worry. She will have to take the baby and move to the father's country, America. My mother does not speak fluent English currently. She wakes up and remembers the dream. She realized it was a dream. She knows it to be real, but still, it is only a dream. Short time later, she runs into an old man. He tells her to take the baby and move to America. This old man tells her she will have three children and a better life. (Not an amazing life but a better life). My mother (So Chom Tok) knows this older man does not know her and does not know she is pregnant with me. My mother realizes this is confirmation from God to leave. She did not want to leave, but she received several confirmations. My mother stepped out on faith does not know what was before her.

My mother and I crossed the ocean to come to America. When I was smaller my mother told me," **The streets were lined with gold."** I have not seen a street made from gold yet. She was not going to kill me, sell me or discard me like trash. She chooses me over her family. My mother comes to a country she believes will be better, but the prejudice still exists no matter what country you live in.

Another man was in love with my mother and had completed three tours to be around her. My mother decides to marry this man. This was the way to America. My mother, not being able to read or write English, took me, and we are coming to America. The man she marries is not prepared to accept us yet. The Army loses all my mother's stuff …all of it. All our clothes, pictures, jewelry, money. I imagine this was a difficult time for the army. There were more than 100,000 Amerasians babies and mothers trying to cross country lines. Identifications and processes are missed.

I did not know until I was forty years of age what all the details were. I found my original birth certificate in 2011, my original Korean birth certificate. In Korea, it is more of a family history (lineage). My birth records state my mother, and I died. Well, in the Korean translation, it says," We are dead the to the family (we are exiled to never return)." The way I got my original birth certificate is I am renewing my passport for my mother and I to travel back to Seoul in October of 2011. My mother gets her passport in three weeks. I received a letter from the state department requesting that I bring everything I have had since childhood to Texas Avenue in Houston, Texas. I am a little "freaked" out. I am scared I will be deported. I speak to someone, and they tell me this is serious. I make the appointment and take everything I can think of since first grade.

I get to the State Department and meet with an agent. The agent tells me there is a problem with my passport and identification. I asked, "What is the problem?" He tells me, "I am either dead or I was stolen as a child. If I cannot provide the documents they need, I will be deported back to South Korea." I called my mother. She calls my youngest uncle and starts to decide for me to go back to Korea. I DON'T SPEAK KOREAN OR WRITE KOREAN. I am panicking. I cannot leave my daughter. It was the Korean birth certificate that was translated by a Korean American "saying "I had died when it really means it, I was dead to the family, exiled. I was assigned a special agent from the State Department." The agent helped me, and I got a passport.

The man I know as my father now was not prepared for my mother and me. He puts us in a single-wide trailer with no water or electricity. My mother made a life for herself and had to give it all up because of me. The guilt I felt over the years was terrible. My mother told me America was rich, "Look, their houses have wheels." This is how my mother looked at her situation. I can tell you in this instance, the streets were not paved with gold; the streets were paved with "dirt." This was a piece of crap trailer. I remember it was very hot in Texas. My mom would take water and put it on the linoleum to keep me cool.

I remember one night or evening, my mom was bawling her eyes out and screaming full of tears and despair. She grabbed the suitcase, and we started down the road. My mother's intentions were to walk or get a ride to Fort Hood, Texas and get her family to get us a plane ticket home from my aunt. While we were walking down this dirt road, a terrible thunderstorm happened. We could not see and the dirt below our feet turned into mud. We were getting stuck walking. My mother, out of despair, turns around, and we go back to our "house on wheels" because we cannot go forward in the storm. If she only knew her life would be a bigger storm in years to come.

The environment is my mother's biological Korean family did not want us because I was a multi-racial child. My biological father did not want me for some reason, and my mother was a foreign woman…. Asian women). I remember my Caucasian grandmother saying, "I do not know why you and Jack (my step-uncle) like these foreign women. We have plenty of good, white American women right here." This woman hates my mom. My stepdad's brother married a Japanese woman. But, to their mother, all Asian women look alike (slanted eyes). To my mom, all women in America look alike, "All big round eyes."

My mom came to America to give me a better life and her life is worse. My stepdad's mother treats her terribly. She could not eat at the table with them. We were not allowed to eat at the table. Fast forward, my mother is pregnant with my baby sister. One night, my stepdad was drinking at grandma's house. Everyone is over getting drunk. My dad wants to go somewhere. My stepdad's cousin wants to go, but she tells my stepdad to put my eight-month-pregnant mom in the back of the Pinto. Yes, a pinto.

They go down the road, and the cousin is upset she must ride in the back. The cousin is telling my stepdad to pull over and make my mother ride in the back. He tries to tell my mother she will have to get in the back. My mother refuses because she is the wife and not to mention she is eight months pregnant. My mom is yelling at him for wanting to make her ride in the back. It becomes very heated, and he starts beating my mom because the cousin is offended. My mom is a foreigner. Why should the Americans ride in the back? He tries to throw her out on the interstate. Hang on, ladies, I am about to tell you what happened. **(I am going to give you a disclaimer, I do not condone violence of any sort but in this case, but I understood it.)**

My mom is one tough cookie. She beats his rear end. Do you hear me, she whooped him. Because of the brutality, she starts having pains. The cousin makes him go to the hospital. The doctor can clearly see what has transpired. The doctor tells my stepdad, "If she dies or the baby dies, you will go to jail. I will make sure of it." I do not know if they called the military police. My mother and my sister are in the hospital. The baby has not moved for three days. Can you imagine the fear, the hurt, the guilt my mother must have felt? Finally, on the fourth day, the baby moves. My mother and my sister are fine.

My mom tells me the story and it makes me cry each time she tells me. She tells me a feeling came over her and gave her strength that she had never known. My mother knew she had to protect my sister and get back to me. Scientifically, this is known as flight or fight. I believe God filled her with the spirit to live.

I know some of you may be in a similar situation or some of you are thinking you would not know what to do in this situation.

As my stepdad starts to sober up and realizes what happened, he understandably feels guilty. He almost killed his own child and wife. You would think this would stop him from drinking alcohol. Nope…. It does not. Then, he returns home to his mother's home. She asks him what happened. He tells her So Chom Tok beat him up and they were fighting. He tells her that he is in the hospital. My despicable grandmother says, "Oh, the **gook** is in the hospital." I did not know what this meant, but from her tone, I could tell the disdain in her voice was not a good word. I asked my aunt. My aunt tells me not to say that word; it has a bad meaning for Asian people like me. I did not know for years what this word really meant. My grandmother is upset that her son was beaten to H_ _LL. (He was scratched up and he had a "chunk" of hair pulled out. This bald spot was there his entire life. As a reminder, every time he looked in the mirror.)

My poor mother, having to put with this prejudice. I am heartbroken each time I think of this for my mother. My mother could have held a grudge, but she said, "Ignorance is everywhere; do not be ignorant Tati". The story is not quite over. My mother is a businessperson who went through two wars. How many times did she have to start from scratch with only the close on her back. (***She lost her family at nine years of age during the Korean War, taking her away from her family and having to take care of her younger brother (youngest uncle) and her baby sister (youngest aunt). A child taking care of two toddler children.***)

Time and several years go by. We moved to a town in Texas. The town was Crockett, Texas. We rented a house that was on quite a bit of land. My mom, being the savvy businesswoman, decides to use the land to grow home-grown vegetables. (We call this farmer's market or Whole Foods now-a-days) Back then, it was known as "You sell vegetables on the side of the road". My mom plants a ton of tomatoes, okra, potatoes, cabbage, beans, and so forth. She is a farmer in all senses of the word. She makes a little produce stand on the side of the road called "Jennie's Produce." (Yes, most Asian women get an American name when they come over to the US. You really don't think they were born as Susan or Kim in Korea, do you?) I got bullied a lot in school because I was poor. My mother made my clothes. (We call this tailored now, but back then, you were poor). I had Caucasian school girls cut off my long hair because they were jealous and mean. They did even cut all of it, they only cut one half so my mom would have to cut off the rest to make it even. Do you think the girls were punished? Of course not. We were poor, foreign, immigrant kids. What people did not realize is my mother worked from late print until fall. She was able to take off during most of our school year with the money she made and saved.

My mother saves enough money to buy us a home in another East Texas town. We also have a store. (You know most Korean have a store………yep, I said it.) We sold gas and BBQ. We are in Texas of course we had BBQ. This was all because of my mother.

Ladies, you can decide what environment you want. Sometimes, the environment you are in is a situation for perseverance and endurance, but you do not know it at the time. God tells my mother to go for a better life, but at this moment, I realize the streets do not have gold, the trailers are only a roof over our heads, and my mother is suffering in silence. There were not as many programs as there are now in the mid to late 70's. There is such a prejudice for minorities and foreign women that she would not have received social assistance.

The moral of this exert is my mother had God in her. She is washed in the blood of Jesus, YHWH, Yahshua. She was beaten but not defeated. Your current environment does not define you or determine your worth.

I am a bi-racial woman, speaking more Spanish than Korean, with the most Southern accent because I grew up in Texas. I am a thicker chick. My environment allowed me to define things I want and do not want in my life. Environment adds characteristics to my personality, but by no means is it a "coffin." When you have God in your life and He is directing your path, He never said it would be easy. He allows you to see the path and provides while you are doing up your path. It took ten years for my mother to have her business.

My pastor explained a scenario one time. The gifts God gives are like shoes. They are your shoes; He gave them to you at birth. Sometimes the shoes hurt your feet and are very difficult to walk or run in, you may outgrow your shoes. Some shoes are comfortable, and you love them for walking or running. God gives you all your shoes. If you put them in the closet and do not use them……. They are still your shoes. They will always be your shoes.

What is a gift? A gift is a thing given willingly to someone without payment. How does God see your gifts? God gives amazing gifts. Through the power of God's spirit, we get access to these incredible gifts for the benefit or plan that is for us all along. There are tangible gifts and supernatural gifts, but they are all a lifetime of work.

Know this, no matter what situation you are in at this moment, you are a princess or prince of a most high God, King of Kings. You are the product of a glorious kingdom.

Chapter 4
"Let us Get into It"

Let us proceed, shall we? First, let us take a glimpse of the timeline for women coming into the modern era. There are numerous roles women attain in society or the workplace. Think of all the roles women play that you know of today. These roles are all common knowledge. Women are (but are not limited to only these roles) Mothers, daughters, friends, homemakers, businesspeople, trendsetters, political women, civil rights activists, farmers, hunters, counselors, educators, healers, influencers, and authors. This is only to name a few categories. I am always intrigued by how many are stereotyped, undervalued, and underestimated. Being underestimated is my favorite. We will get into that a little later in the book. During my career, I have had three stereotypes that seem to come out more than others. I will share how I look at these stereotypes. When I speak and bring these characters in focus, people get a kick out of them but, then realize they are more real than they could have ever imagined. When you read about them, your first thought may be, "What da'heck?" It will make sense".

Stereotype Number One

Happy Homemaker

This is how I got to know Happy Homemaker in my career. I was in my early 20's and working with an exceptionally large retailer on the supply chain distribution side of the business. Really, this was my first big job. I did not understand how women were viewed, but I was a quick study, and I learned very quickly this was a male-dominated environment. When I started with the company, I was an hourly associate unloading, loading, picking, being a clerk in the receiving office, traffic, and every department in the distribution center. As an hourly associate, the company was very pro associate. I thought to myself, I want to retire here.

I had to move to Central Texas to start up our third building in our company's venture of acquisition. When I got to Central Texas, the company hired new managers from outside the company to assist with the venture. Most (not all) of these men did not grow up in the culture of this large retailer. It was as if we flipped a switch; metrics were the only thing that mattered. There was absolutely no work-life balance, and that was the normal expectation. You will eat, breathe, sleep, and die for this company. If the associate did not make 100% productivity by the end of the 90-day probationary period, he or she would be separated from the company. Even if the associate was at 97% or 97% productivity. "IT HAD TO BE 100%." It did not seem logical to me. I mean 97% or 98% in school is an A+. My common-sense, logical mind thought it was "stupid" to terminate someone for 98% productivity. Has the company not ever heard, "98% loaf of bread is better than no loaf of bread?" I found it quickly; common sense is not so common. I went to my manager and debated my case. Could we not work with the associate to get them to 100% instead of starting over? With a deep voice and poking out his chest, he let me know if was 100% or nothing. If they cannot produce 100% the associate does not need to be with our company. If I could not do what he needed I did not need to work for the company. What a fool! The original reason I chose to get into management was because I did not like how management treated their associates. At this moment, I realized I needed to be a lot higher in the company if I was going to make a positive impact on associates and supervision. At this moment, I have two hundred associates working on order selection. I turned my two hundred associates in one year. I had to do my job. It was my least favorite thing to do. An associate going home telling a partner, wife, or husband, I lost my job today because my manager fired anyone not at 100%. The manager would say, "I did not fire them, they fired themselves."

For the most part, I was always an outstanding associate and usually exceeded expectations as a leader. I did not realize that people learn at a different pace because this was not the "bill of goods" this company was selling. I never had an issue running my business. Meeting or exceeding metrics came very naturally to me. Deep down inside, I said, **"There has to be a better way."** I read all the Franklin Covey, Dale Carnagie, Zig Zigler books and more books.

About a year later, I was moved to a different department and a different part of the business with a different leader. My new Operations Manager was a Lieutenant Colonel in the Army. We will call this person Lt, Cornel for the sake of the book.

One evening towards the end of shift he called me to the office and wanted to talk with me. I had no idea what this meeting was about. I thought it would be something regarding a task in the distribution center.

He starts the conversation by letting me know that he has never seen anyone who runs numbers like me, and I execute better than most men he had in the Army. (Is this a compliment comparing me to men in the Army?) I believe it was supposed to be a compliment of sorts. He continued the speech, "I am better than most of the guys in the distribution center. His tone is different, not smooth. Then, he proceeds to tell me …." With that being said, you are a "bitch" to work with and it's difficult to work for you." "Your guys hate working for you. Associates do not want to work with me because they are afraid to lose their jobs." I quietly sit there listening. A few minutes go by. He asked if I had anything to say, did I have any thoughts? Boy, did I have a few thoughts for him. I could feel my cheeks turning red, and my ears started to get warm. I was composed. I did not want to lose my job. I kept it professional. I told him, "I am not here to make friends; the company pays me "X" amount of dollars to protect their interest and get the job done. The other manager I worked with before you, Lt. Colonel, made me and other supervisors fire anyone not at 100% productivity, and we had no room to maneuver. It's his way or this highway. Lt. Cornel agreed and said that guy is an "A__HOLE." I am perplexed at this moment. I am thinking to myself, if you managers know he is a "butt head," why do we tolerate him in our company? Lt. Cornel says, you do not understand yet, but there are a lot of politics the higher you go. He tells me if I could be a little "softer" and take a different approach it would be better. (The first thing I think is, "Do I look like a 5'8" rabbit?") The next thought I have silently in my mind is, "Are you stupid?" My mother is Korean, and my father is a military veteran, and you want me to be softer. Why can I not come to work and do my job?) I replied, in a softer but more sarcastic voice, "You want me to come in here and work all day with grown men and be their mother; **I am not Happy Homemaker!**" Lt. Cornel said, "You might want to be if you plan to get ahead in this business." What I did not realize at the time was that it is part of my responsibility to be kind and empathic to people. But this is not what I was taught in the early 1990s. It was the end of my shift. I sat in my truck for a moment and cried. I was so mad that I was working my butt off with these long 16-hour days, making all my metrics and I get told I should be softer to get ahead. How dare this little 5'6" man tells me I am a (b-word that rhymes with witch). Apparently, being an" a. hole" is ok. All these grown-ass men need to be coddled. Gees Louise. I went home and read in my Bible. I wanted to see how the Bible portrayed women. What did God think of women and how did He utilize women?

This was the first time I wanted to understand God's role for women. Think about Ester in the Bible. She had a life of poverty and living day to day. God had a plan for her and allowed a blessing that she was not aware of until later. Her path was already designed.

What kept playing in my mind over and over all weekend was the remark about getting ahead. After I got home, I was over the phrase that, I was bitchy. I have been called the worst, ladies………. **Truth**- I prayed and prayed. I called my mother. My mother tells me to listen to my boss; he is my boss. You are so stubborn. (My mother still says the exact same thing for every boss I have ever had…still to this day) Maybe I needed my mom to level-set me, or it was hearing her voice.

I do not know what came over me, but a peace. It was like logic came into my brain. I said to myself, "Let me think about this for a moment. I prayed, "God, you sent me feedback and I did not like it at all. If I have a lesson here, let me see it. I looked up a Happy Homemaker. My first thought was BC for bull crap.

Happy Homemaker was my first comparison for a stereotype. In this moment, I decided I wanted to improve my situation and move up for a few reasons. 1) I want to treat people and leaders better than I was treated, 2) I want to develop people in a different way, and 3) I want to give direction and make policy that is better than what I see currently with this company.

Stereotype Number Two

Errand Girl

Errand girl came later in the life of my career. I was at a women's workshop. The company brought in a Women's Support Image group. The company evaluated the way we looked and how we managed ourselves. The company will give you feedback on your professionalism and what you may want to do to improve your appearance. I was told I should color my grey "skunk stripe" in the middle of my head. The one thing they told all of us to do was make sure we were aware of our surroundings. We never know who is watching us, and when we are out and about, people who know us, but we do not know them. I thought this was an interesting statement. We had a wonderful leader, and towards the end of the meeting, she gave me a miniature figure of" Snow White". She asked me if a reminder was. I had to figure this out. It was driving me crazy. I decided to analyze this statement.

Think about Snow White and her character. A beautiful story. A beautiful princess who takes care of little men. She sweeps for them (cleaning up their mess), cooks for them, tends to the cottage, washes their clothes, bakes for them, sews their clothes, pampers them, consoles them, making them nice. She runs all the errands. She is even a therapist of sorts. The men go to work every day, and she tends to the cottage and anything dealing with homemaker duties. The seven men have different personalities. The more I thought about this, the more I realized the following things. Most male figures can relate to having an Errand Girl or Happy Homemaker in their lives. The men have all these temperaments and personalities and expect women to be happy or content taking care of them. The next thing I realize is the men like well put together women.

I decided to do my own test. For several years after, when I had an audit or something I wanted to get across, I would wear "RED" lipstick. I was going to test my theory with this character. I worked for different companies where were had third-party auditors came in and evaluated different things. On those days I would wear a little more make up and my RED lipstick. Anyone who knew of my red lipstick test realized would giggle a little until I got the results back. I got the best scoring audits, even perfect scores. I never mentioned it to the men, but my ladies knew, and we would test the theory. I once had an executive vice president say, "It must be luck to me." I thought to myself, "Buddy, it is not luck!!! I would do an excellent job without my red lipstick, but it became an amusing conversation with my female teams. Our Errand Girl is a reminder that there is still a bias in the workplace. It may be unassuming, and the male figures do not intend to recognize this, but it is subconscious. The men cannot help it. It is hardwired in them. I would be invited to come skiing in Vermont, or if I were in their area, they would love to take me out to eat to appreciate the relationship. Of course, I would never take any of the offers. I would prove my test to my female leaders. I would give them a figurine just like the leader gave me. I am sure the figurine I got was more to remind me to be composed and well put together and to smile when we were not happy inside. I have the figurine to remind me and other female leaders that this is still a male-dominated environment to always use your ability to empower, influence, and take care of people even if they are grumpy, unhappy, lazy, and so forth. We have more ability, empowerment, and influence than we realize. Sometimes, we got to' put on a little red lipstick.

Stereotype Number Three

Wonder Woman

This is the stereotypical character that we can relate to the most. I feel in today's modern age; we all feel like Wonder Woman. Wonder Woman was my favorite character when I was young. A fact you may not know is DC Comics made Wonder Woman a person who could wield Thor's hammer. She can weld and hold Thor's hammer because she is worthy. **We women are worthy**. She is equal in integrity and virtue. She has a magic lasso that makes people tell the truth. Diana (Wonder Woman) has an invisible jet to take her anywhere she wants to go. She is from a strong line of women warriors and leaders who can do anything a male warrior can do. If you ever saw the TV show "Wonder Woman," Lynda Carter as Diana was a professional. She would twirl around and turn into this fierce woman who could do anything. She had to hide her identity. What I found interesting is the closest man to her could not see her worth or powers and did not recognize she was this amazing "Wonder Woman. "Are any of you close to a male figure, right next to him, and he does not see you are a Wonder Woman? Fact- this happens every day. We women hope they will see how great we are and recognize our potential. Wonder Woman is supportive, domineering, beautiful, and takes care of other women because she comes from a great line of Amazonians. Her father is Zeus. He is the god of gods in Greek mythology. Often, this is the scenario. Here we are in our daily grind multitasking, getting it done, holding down the fort, making everyone else's lives better but not our own life.

My dear ladies, there is one who will always see your worth. He is our Father God, (YHWH, Yahshua, Jesus). You are the daughter of our REAL GOD. He may have many names, but he is the father, son, and holy spirit. Father God has given you miraculous powers and gifts. You have an invisible jet to take you anywhere you want to go in life and in your career. The physical person right next to you may not see your worth, but God knew when you were conceived, and he knows every hair on your head and every tear you shed. Our Father God sees your worth and will make others see your worth. You will use your gifts for good, not evil. You will be supported by others because no one can control your path other than God.

Can you see the three characters and the stereotypes within them? Can you relate to any of the three characters or are you relating to all three characters? You cannot wait for man (fleshly) to see you. Allow God to show the world who you are and what great talents you possess. Allow Him to give you your gifts (your shoes).

Chapter 5
"Characters We Have to Deal with on a Daily Basis"

These characteristics we must deal with daily or sometime during our life. These characteristics can apply to your workplace or your immediate circle of people. No one wants to talk about these characters, but we are going to talk about them and how to deal with them. We will not allow them to take away your focus, your energy, or your joy.

One, there is still plenty of misogyny in the workplace and society. Men that still cannot act right in the workplace or outside the workplace even though sexual harassment is taught and discussed everywhere. This goes for women too. I know we all go through sexual harassment training at work, and we are here how it is unacceptable in society. Truth – It still happens a million times a day to a million different women and men. Second, the double standard still exists. Yes, we have laws to protect us against discrimination. Truth- It is alive and well. Women are still paid less than their male counterparts, and we lose out on promotions because of the double standard. We really are not allowed to discuss monetary compensation in the workplace. This tells me we cannot discuss my self-worth like I want to in the workplace. Third and lastly, Prejudice is still a real thing. It is a living, breathing entity. It may be more in the form of cliques, or there are underlying things we cannot talk about. Yes, we have federal laws prohibiting prejudice. **Truth** - It is still there. In some instances, it has gotten better over the years, but it is still there, and we have all experienced a version of it in our day-to-day experiences. Additionally, these characters are working against us.

Character 1

The Jealous Person

If you are in God's light and receiving favor and blessings, the jealous character will always show up. Have you ever had a person that just hates you because? You have not done anything to this person, but he/she is so jealous of you. You cannot figure out why. You have a couple of options. You can have a sincere one-on-one conversation and find out why. You can look at it from a Godly point of view. Do not covet your neighbor or your neighbor's things. But human nature cannot help it.

When you walk with God, people will always be jealous of you. It is because they do not understand what a relationship with God brings you. The jealous person cannot figure it out. They just do not care for you at all. It is the favor and joy you have.

How do you deal with this person? You continue to be yourself. Set clear boundaries for you and this person. Do not allow jealousy to become gossip or a topic of conversation. Continue to be kind. If the situation does not improve, then you may have to confront the issue. Know that anything you do may not help the situation. You live in accordance with what God would expect.

Character 2

"The Lazy Person"

This person never meets deadlines or does their portion of the workload. This person will call you twenty-four hours before a project deadline is due and ask you to help them because they have been so busy. We are all busy, it is called life and work. The person who makes it to the meeting tries to propose as if they worked on this project as much as you did. You are in a meeting, and you cannot believe the words coming out of this person's mouth. You are offended he/she wants to appear as if they are a hard worker. You do not say anything, but you leave the meeting frustrated. This person has a repeat pattern. You can manage it by allowing this to continue to happen. This could be a friend, co-worker, spouse, or significant other. This person does not believe in sharing tasks with you. It may be because of a double standard that is unconscious, or it may be how this person is brought up. How many times have you worked, come home, cooked dinner, and washed clothes while your spouse or partner is watching TV or already in bed? You can call them out in the meeting or wake them up. You can manage it differently by according to how God would have you act. This is what God says about the laziness of a person.

How to deal with a lazy person? First, you do not stop being and level of work ethic you have each and every day. It is easier to say, "I am not going to do the work because he/she is not doing the work". God has given you the ability to be fruitful. Do not squander that ability because of someone else. Laziness is a lack of motivation or a lack of interest in something. See if you can find what motivates this person and help them become more interested. This may change how they look at work.

Character 3

"The Ghost Person"

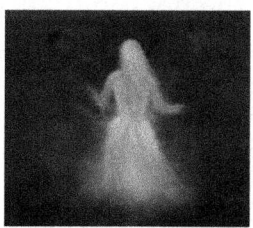

This person is called a "ghost person" because they are never around physically. They exist, you know of them, but they are in a different realm and not present in your life. You never see them. One minute, they are right there, and poof, the next minute, they are gone. It may be a worker never comes to work or an absent parent. You end up doing your workload and theirs, like so many single mothers. The leaders do not address this issue. You are thinking, "I am the only one that sees what is going on …. when is this person going to get some accountability?" The leaders allow this person to get away with being absent. In our daily lives, this may be a parent now showing up to help with the children. You may be trying to work and go to school and the person is supposed to come over while you study or attend class. The person never shows up. They are not there for you. How you deal with someone who is never there to deal with you can be frustrating and complicated.

How to deal with the "ghost" person? The first thing is to know God is always with you. When you have God, He can be there for you. God can place people in your life to assist you. At some point, you must accept the boundaries and the truth about this person. They will not decide to be there for you. It is not in their DNA. If the person wants to be there for you, he or she will be there. You cannot stop prioritizing the things that are important to you. You will need to realize what is important to you and how to deal with the absence of the person, spouse, significant other, or co-worker. God is never absent. Get a schedule of daily or weekly activities. When I was a single mom, I knew I meal prepped on the weekends for the next two weeks. This enabled me to come home, prepare meals for my daughter, and work on my master's degree after she went to bed.

Character 4

"Ole' Fluff and Stuff Person"

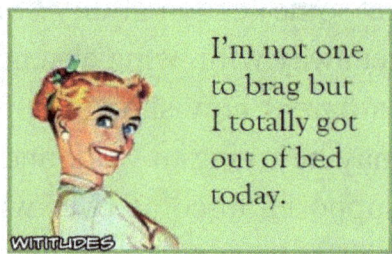

This person is larger than life. They pretend to be better or greater than you. This person is of little importance in your day-to-day life but tries to show up as if they are more important than you. They may walk in with an expensive purse they cannot afford. It is all about the show. They may even appear whimsical to leadership. They may be boastful about themselves or the agenda they are trying to push. They are trifling (yes, I said it, trifling). This person makes a mountain out of molehill. Whatever is important to them MUST be equally important to you. They are a performer or a pretender. They attempt to make people believe they are larger than life or they may have prestige. They will try to appear they are dominate over you. They get on your nerves. It makes you want to "roll your eyes" at them. Have you met anyone that fits this description? All day long…... if you are single and dating you see quite a few "fluff and stuff" people who believe they are larger than life. What should be done about these characters? What does God say about this person. God does not care for people who are boastful or full of pride.

How to deal with this person? God encourages us to be dependable, reliable, and humble. These characteristics are how you deal with a person like this on a day-to-day basis. Walk away, do not engage in prideful (spiteful behavior.

Character 5

"Smoke and Mirrors Person"

The smoke never allows you to get a clear view or a clear reading of this person. It makes it difficult to see their true character. The mirrors make them seem like they have more to offer but there is no substance. The mirror is there for them to look at themselves because they are the most important ego. They love to be in the limelight or the center of attention. This person makes leadership or people believe they know more than they really know. They will talk a good game, they are pretenders. This person is very manipulative; they are deceivers. They will be in meetings rambling about nothing, but it sounds good. You finish the meeting, and you think, what did he/she say? Nothing, absolutely nothing. This person will attempt to use big words to sound smarter. The person will refer to experiences that may not exist. This person will be a certain way around executive leaders, but around you, they are condescending and belittling. This person will undermine your work or create a situation to pigeonhole you. When dealing with this character you will see they try to create a confusing situation or create a situation that is not what it seems. When it comes to the actual work, he or she cannot do the work needed. They will convince someone to do it for them versus being collaborative and assisting. They will want to contradict you to make you look "stupid." Yes, I said it. Yes, stupid is an ugly word, but it is true. They may bounce around from department to department to keep the ruse going.

How do you deal with this type of person? God will give you discernment to see these types of characters. The supernatural gift of discernment allows you to see or detect evil when it is around you, which is in Corinthians 1:12. The lighter gift of discernment is your intuition or when you get the odd feeling in your stomach. You will be able to see right through the situation. God will want you to distance yourself from these manipulators. You do not want to be guilty by association. You may have to deal with this person because of work or a relationship, but you must have your guard up and do no fall the lies. Ask God to reveal things to you to protect you and He will.

There are more characters than these six characters. If you have encountered any of these six people, you know exactly what I am discussing and if I were a betting woman, you can picture a face with each characteristic. You may see one person with multiple characteristics. These may apply to co-workers, leaders, family members, or friends (acquaintances). For me, these are the six that make you want to punch them in the throat. Yes, I said, "Punch them in the throat." As a disclaimer, I do not condone violence of any sort and I would never act such transgressions, but I surely understand at times. Dealing with people like this day after day can take a toll on your mind, body, emotions, and spirit. When you have a close relationship with God, you get a shield of armor for protection and sight to see past the smoke and mirrors. You must learn to be acquainted with this type of individual and only interact with minimal and necessary presence.

Character 6

"The Backstabbing Person"

All the characters discussed earlier have an impact on our lives and feelings. The backstabber is surely the one that can hurt the most. You believe and trust this person with your emotions, your time, and your feelings. This character is a manipulator and an abuser. This one hurts you because you are invested in them in friendship or working relationships. This character will talk behind your back or use things against you for their benefit. They will be your acquaintance to lure information from you or set up a situation that will benefit them in the future. This person is out to justify their actions and only wanting their success. They use backstabbing because they are insecure or inferior in their social or work situation.

How do you deal with a backstabbing person. You must always remain calm and courageous. The backstabber only has power over you if "your back is turned". Do not turn your back. The next thing is you need to have this person out of your life as much as possible. Keep your information and details about your life close to your chest. Let us say it is a person a work. You do have to have interactions with them, but you will need to keep it simple, short, and polite. Not offering any more information that is necessary to the work at hand. Never give them another chance to burn you or stab you in the back. God expects you not to do the same thing and to walk a higher road. Let God take care of a backstabbing person. His vengeance is more than anything you could ever think of to do to a person. Give it to God. Allow God to make that person your footstool.

Chapter 6
"The Right Mindset- The G Element"

The God Element

Now, that we have discussed several themes from understanding that being a product of your environment does not determine your environment, we have talked about three types of women I have experienced, the six types of people that you encounter in your day-to-day lives, and how to think about the situation. We are now going to learn about the "Right Mindset, the God Element."

What is an element? What is the definition of an element?

Element- a part or aspect of something abstract, especially one that is essential or characteristic.

How does God define an element?

Element-In its primary sense, as denoting the FIRST PRINCIPLE or constituents of things.

Do you see the difference? The worldly definition says, "a part or aspect". While God says, **"It the first principle"**.

This is where you will start your transformation. Understanding how the world defines an element and how God defines an element. Believe me, it will not be easy. This will be a difficult, long, and exhausting transformation. The transformation will not come overnight, next week, or even next year. But I promise, if you do this; nothing will stand in your way, and you will overcome and move forward to "GET AHEAD."

Fundamental factors are always discussed in self-help books, leadership books, seminars, or podcasts. We keep asking why we cannot move ahead, get deliverance, or the promotion you deserve. We pray for help, blessings, or relief. When we exercise (well, when you may exercise), it is always about building a strong core. We hear in the medical field that our guts are important because, in our stomachs, we fight diseases. Our gut takes all our food and has all the ingredients to break down our food and give us what we need.

Faith and the relationship you have with God is fundamental. Faith fights diseases and sickness like our gut does. This principle applies with the right mindset to establish a God element, your strong core. The mindset is how to set up the fundamentals that will govern your thoughts and behaviors and start to unlock your path. The mind is a strong organ that allows rationality and learning to come into your body. The God element. What is an element.

Let us start with truth and understanding who gives you all your blessings. Having a covenant with God and understanding His Son is the only path to move forward or to move ahead. The fleshly meaning of covenant. It is defined as an agreement between them as a contract.

In God's truth covenant is a bond. God sees covenant as a foundational binding agreement between God and the person. In Thessalonians 1, 2:2, even after we had suffered before, and we are spiritually treated as Philippe as you know we were bold in God to speak to you the gospel God in much Conflict. Be assured of God's saving work, Psalms 20, 1-5.

I was brought up in a Christian home. My mother is a God-fearing woman. I did not understand her personal relationship with God until I was much older. I understood my mother was more blessed than most.

How do you shift into this relationship with God? Having this personal, sincere relationship will allow you to be proactive and protected, allow you to look at things through a much different lens, understand your purpose, and have a reputation that will precede you. We will discuss this a little later in the book. Establish your covenant with God, according to God's way not the fleshly, modern way. In His word, He clearly tells you He hears you. He will grant you according to your heart's desire and fulfill all your purpose. May the Lord fulfill your petition. You must ask Him what your purpose is in a sincere and humble manner. You must talk to Him as if you are talking to a person sitting right next to you. You can be vulnerable with Him. Your vulnerability shows Him you are open, and you trust Him. Ask God to reveal your path. I was twenty-eight years old when God started showing me my path. I asked Him; and I told God I wanted to have a covenant with Him. Like the covenant he has with Israel. I wanted all the grace and favor He promised in His word.

The problem was I did not know how to listen or how to hear from God. I came across two books, Battlefield of the Mind and How to Hear from God written by Joyce Meyers. After I read these two books, it was like a telephone installed in my mind that had a direct pathway to God. Look, I was a little doubtful, but I did not have anything to lose. I learned that God gives me confirmation in 3s. It took me some time to realize how He was speaking to me. This is how I know it is God telling things. This may not be what He has for you. To this day I still get confirmation in 3s. Having a covenant enables Faith. Fear is the absence of Faith. The covenant and faith will allow the next you to have the ability to Sow and reap gifts, rewards that you can never imagine.

Chapter 7
"The Principles of Sowing and Reaping"

We all know a little about physics. What goes up must come down and what goes down will go up. All actions have an opposite and equal reaction. Well, in God's peace, we have principles of "sowing and reaping." All the effort you put in will have a reaction. If you are not in God's element, you are not in the Godly mindset, thinking there may not be a purpose for you. What are you creating in the universe? The purpose for sowing and reaping? You may not know this in your current situation; sowing and reaping is exactly like planting our garden; it takes a minute to see the harvest. We will look at four principles.

One

Take Responsibility

You have heard many times before in self-help books, leadership books, or different podcasts. We should take responsibility for ourselves. But no one really tells you what kind of responsibility. Many times, it is responsibility in the flesh or how man sees responsibility. Know when I speak of flesh or "man," it is a reference to earthly (not man versus women). In the 21st century responsibility is much different than the original connotation in the Godly sense. Our Godly responsibility was established way before what we know as corporate or social responsibility. Today, we are to take responsibility for ourselves and our actions in a manly or fleshly sense. We must be responsible only to ourselves first. In this sense, I want you to understand Godly value, the responsibility for the way he created you. In the Godly element, you have responsibilities to understand your talents. You must be responsible for allowing God to lead you in life and your movements to achieve what you need and what you desire. You are to be responsible to look out for others when they cannot look out for themselves. Be responsible to know your limits, but understand God has no limits for you. Be actionable to know that you are in his favor and love.

There are no limits that will keep you from not moving forward.

Two

Redefine Your Mistake

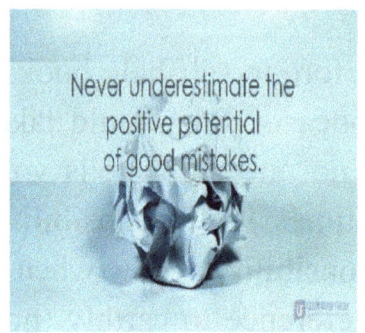

Everyone makes mistakes. Hence, the phrase, "I knew then what I know now." Mistakes happen every day, all day long, by millions of people. Mistakes are natural because we are "sinners". Sounds harsh, but we were designed to have flaws, to make mistakes, and to sin. This is the truth. This is the gift of free will. We do not think about being a sinner or we do not talk about all our sins. We think or say to ourselves, "I am only human". Exactly, we are human with all our faults and mistakes. Rectify your mistakes, learn to re-define your mistakes. You are thinking in this moment, "What is she talking about? Redefine your mistakes. We conceive mistakes in distinct categories, much like sin. If a person steals or lies, it is not as bad as adultery or coveting your neighbor? "Sin is Sin."

We must think about our mistakes the same way. A mistake is a mistake. There are no mistakes worse than other mistakes. Society makes us believe this way. If I lie at work, which leads to a mistake, or I actually owned up to a mistake.... either way, it is a mistake. Each mistake has a negative impact whether the mistake is small or large. It is a mistake, PERIOD. What could we have done differently? Not like about the mistake. We must give equal weight to mistakes. If I cause an office disruption, it surely cannot be as bad as a network mistake. Dear, you cause a mistake to have a negative impact on situations and people. We need to be proactive and anticipate mistakes to avoid them altogether. Much like avoiding a sinful situation. I am married; I choose to avoid any situation that may have me in a situation of potential cheating. I do not go out or frequent bars or clubs. I make the free will choice for not allowing myself to be tempted.

You must be careful and selective in the actions you take because your actions leave invisible fingerprints in the fabric of time in the universe. The action(s) you do today will have a cause and effect later in time. If you could run a simulation on our actions.... wow, would that not be the perfect thing to have to set our future. In simple, modern times our actions always have consequences. You have heard the analogy that if you throw a pebble in it has ripples that go across the surface, but what people do not see is the ripples are deep below. The phrase we hear is the "Golden Rule". Treat others as you would want to be treated. The principle goes back to Biblical times. We rebranded the phrase to fit our modern situation.

Three

Repent and Ask for Forgiveness

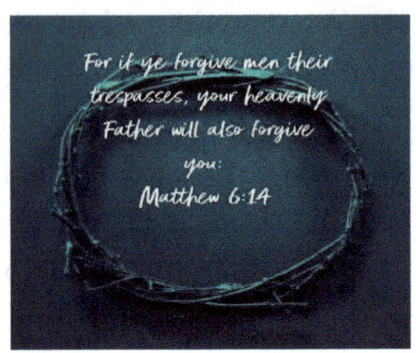

We should desire not to repeat a mistake. Forgiveness is not for the other person. Forgiveness is for us. Define your mistake and define the outcome. God gave his Son. He forgave us of all our sins. The concept of forgiveness is part of your covenant with God, showing Him that you recognize what He did for you. You are forgiving mistakes, and sin is you recognizing the unbelieve love and blessings. You may need to forgive yourself. Forgiveness does not feel good all the time because life is not fair. You do everything you are supposed to, and why is it you that has been forgiven? It is because you are showing our Heavenly Father you have faith; he will take the hurt, pride, and disappointment and turn it into good for you. You are stepping out on Faith, which shows God you will do as he wishes, not what the "flesh" wishes to do.

Psalms 130: Out of the depths I have cried to you O'Lord; Lord hear my voice! Lend Your ear to be attentive to the voice of my supplications. If You, Lord should mark iniquities O' Lord who shall stand? But there is Forgiveness with YOU. I wait for the Lord, my soul waits. Andin His work I do hope. My soul waits for the Lord more than those who watch for the morning. Yes, more than those who watch for the morning. O Isreal, hope in the Lord for with the Lord there is mercy, and with Hin is ABUNDANT REDEMPTION.

Four

"Put Your Seed in the Right Ground"

Let us go a little deeper, shall we? Yes, we want to sow good seeds with amazing rewards and bountiful harvests. You genuinely believe in your heart you are sowing seeds with good actions. But you cannot figure out why, for the life of you, you cannot get ahead or move forward. The bills keep coming, promotions pass you buy, you can tell your boss does not like you no matter what you do. I can tell you are fighting a fight every day. It is a war on you. I am not endorsed or sponsored by this person, but her book

Battlefield of the Mind by Joyce Meyers is one of the foundation books to set your spirit right.

Have you ever considered you may be sowing your seeds in the wrong ground. You must put your seeds on the right ground. Yes, I hit you with a double tap. It is not only the fact you have to have good seeds, but you must put your good seeds in the right place.

Your seed(s) need all the right elements to go and bring a harvest. You must know that the seed must die first before it can grow into what you want. Your worldly (fleshy-manly) life must die before you can grow into God's light. He will make sure your seed is in the right soil, with the right love, water, sunlight, and all the nutrients you need to bring a bountiful harvest. Much like a plant, you must know what season you are in with God. Allow God to take away your burden. All you must do is invest in yourself by allowing God to invest in you and grow your future. Truth - You have heard, "Oh, keep doing what you are doing. You will get there someday." Truth - If you must replant then replant.

God (YHWY, Yahshua, Jesus) had me in different seasons. What I did not understand is I thought I was planting my seed but all along God was planting his seed in me. I am thinking at the time I am sowing a seed, but the was in me to do better things.

I was working for a company that was not so great. Prejudice, chauvinistically dominated by men. While I was there, I had a young girl collaborating with me. I could see her potential. We will call her "B" for the sake of the story. She came over to my department to work each time she got a chance. I gave her some advice about her career and told her she should explore getting human resources experience and even attain a human resources degree. A human resource degree is versatile. I left the company. Little did I know ten years later; she called me to tell me she was ready to come work for me again. She tells me she did what I told her and is working in human resources for an exceptionally large hospital network in metropolitan area. She bought a home in Richmond, Texas (outside the Houston area). She was recently divorced and is now a single mother. God knows I had been there like her. She has a wonderful family who decide to help her with her son, and she moves to San Antonio, Texas to work with me. She was still paying for her home in Richmond, Texas and paying for an apartment in San Antonio, Texas while being a single mom. I had sown a seed with her and now she was going to sow a seed with me. She has her apartment and sees her son as much as she can on her off days. Some time passes, I accept another position to grow my career. My assistant director takes over my building. The director gets another new position in Houston. The distribution center is in Richmond, Texas. The Director offered "B" a job with him and his organization. Her home is Richmond, Texas. Did you hear me? This young, brilliant woman sowed a seed years ago. "B" grew her career, experience, and monetary value. God saw this long before she and I even realized what was going to happen.

"B" stepped out with faith and God provided. I could even make this up if I tried. I saw something amazing in this young woman. I realized my purpose was to work in God's order to help her. Not me. I did not realize this until I found out she was moving back to work with the Director whose distribution center was in Richmond, Texas. If she had never called me, she would have never met this man who eventually took her back home. Everything she went through. Moving, having her son taken care of by her loving family while she is working toward moving ahead. How long was this period? It was about fourteen years give or take a little. From the time I met her in Houston to the time she moved back to Richmond. Seasons are not always quick. Sometimes, they are long.

Sowing and reaping take a long time to attain a bountiful harvest. Do not be discouraged. It takes **perseverance and endurance.**

Chapter 8
Perseverance and Endurance

What is the definition of perseverance and endurance? Are they the same or similar?

The definition of perseverance is continued effort to achieve something despite difficulties, failures, or opposition.

The definition of endurances is the fact or power of enduring a difficult process or situation without giving way.

This can be tough. It is not easy, and you cannot do it alone. Perseverance goes hand in hand with endurance. At times you will wonder how much longer before I see my blessings, your purpose, your promotion, or you are getting ahead.

Truth- You must persevere and endure forever. Every day of your life, you will preserve and endure heartbreak, doubt, depression, and tiredness, and you will want to throw your hands in the air and give up at times. To have perseverance and the ability to endure takes faith. Faith grew incrementally, similar to a 401K. It goes over time and takes a very long time to mature. Too long is ask me. With time and endurance, your faith will grow (just like a 401K). Sometimes, there are bad investments, and you lose some of your 401K. This is why your faith must be strong, and you must make the right investment…. your investment in God. Faith always pay dividends. Perseverance is slightly modified in the 21st century in books such as "Getting Ahead or Having Power". Think about how God thinks of perseverance and endurance. We all know the Biblical story of Mosses, with the Israelites wandering the desert for forty years.

What you must understand is God allows things to happen because he is omniscient (all-seeing, all-knowing). There are things He will see that you will never see coming because it is God who will put you on your path (not man). Humor me and do this one exercise. Put the book down after you read this. Close your eyes. Take your hands and put them side by side, right in front of your face, almost touching your nose. Then, open your eyes. You cannot see past your hands (they are too thick and solid). Now, put down one hand. You can only see partly what is in front of you. We cannot see what is in front of us. God is looking down below and sees everything in front of us. He will even let you go down a path that you think is right, but it is not right. God will always bring you back to the right path. He will have to move obstacles out of your way or get people to help clear the path so you can get back to where He wants you. Much like the Israelites, they did not mind doing it for a while, but as humans, we grow weary, and we get tired. Having focus and purpose takes a long time. God would show the Israelites their path, but they would stray. We are not different today. We do not mind enduring and preserving for a little bit, but we want results when we think it has been too long. Having faith allows you to have perseverance, endurance, and will not allow you to be a victim. Yes, I said it, "You will not be a victim."

I am going to reference a TV series on Prime Video. The TV series is named "Lioness", written by Taylor Sheridan with an all-star cast. This series is based on a program that sent female soldiers into Iraq. It takes the two main characters. The commanding officer and her pupil begin a professional relationship. In the series, a young girl with a tough environment stubble her way into a Marine recruiting office while running for her life. The marine sees what she has been through but sees something within her (potential). The young girl becomes a marine. The Marine core notices she has talents and there is something special about her. She takes a job with the CIA. During her testing, her commanding officer has her taken offsite, where she is beaten and tortured. The CIA operatives doing the torture and beating think she has had too much, and they might kill her.

The Commanding officer tells the men, I need to see her breaking point so I will know when to pull her out and how much time I have. The men stop the exercise because it is too much in their eyes.

God is much like this scene of this series. God will put us through testing to see how much we can take before He pulls us out. You will be beaten and tortured, and (man) will not believe in your perseverance and endurance. You will do what you must, and when you need God to be there, He will be. In the last show of season one, the young female marine has her first mission. She is left on an island by herself to complete her mission. The mission happens and she must get off the island. She does not know if help will be there. The bad men are shooting bullets at her and chasing her. She must find her way off the island. She must take unexpected paths and run out of faith. Her commanding officer is there with reinforcements to get her. I imagine glimpsing into her mind, running blind, having things come at you that could stop you instantly. But she keeps running and the bullets keep missing her. God will do the same thing for you. As the day-to-day bullets come at you, trying to take away your joy, purpose, and ability to move ahead, the dreadful things will just barely miss you for some reason. You must keep running until you are directed where to go if you have not seen the series watch it and pay attention to the parts I am referencing. They will hit a chord with you.

When you walk in your covenant and perseverance with God, He will give you an unremarkable ability to endure. God has no limits on how he will bless you. Have perseverance to serve God. He will move behind the scenes to have people to help you, and the people are there to stand in your way of His blessings. You will not believe who He puts in front of you and who He removes for your sake. Remember the exercise: you cannot see on the other side of your hands, but God looks down and sees every path. He knows the paths where he must send help to pull you back over. There are distinct roles in life we must play. You must be the right role and the right role model according to God.

Think about a mound of ants. Somehow, they know exactly where to go. They are hard-wired that way. If you take your show and rub out their path, they get a little frenzy attempting to find their path back to the right track to get home. In minutes, they are back on track but there is a new path, but it leads them right back home. We are remarkably similar in this way. We are all hardwired for God. But sometimes, someone rubs out of our path. We freak out, we experience distress, and we are lost. We are lost for a period. But God always brings us back.

Chapter 9
"Role Model - Protecting your Reputation"

In today's society, it is all about, "How am I going to get mine?" "Do whatever you have to do to be on top." My questions for you are.... 1) "On top of what?" 2) "Get you what?"

You can be on top of a pile of "poo". I mean, that is on top .... of something. Then you are going to get "your what?" You can get revenge, or you can be one of the six characters I listed in the previous chapter.

Ladies, you must think about how you move ahead and rise through life. It is important how you play the game. People do not talk much about reputation anymore. How do you become a good role model for other women and men? There are plenty of role models in society with bad reputations. I ask you this, "How do you become the right role model for women?" There is a difference. I praise God my mother was the best role model I could have ever had. I have a best friend. Sometimes we talk often sometimes not for a long time. Each time I call her it is as if we talked yesterday. She brilliant and beautiful which a very successful career. She is an amazing role model. Look, we have all done things we are not proud of in life. God knows I have my moments in my past. The past is exactly where it needs to stay in your past. When God looks at your past, He sees everyone who has hurt you, made you cry, or done wrong to you. God also looks at everyone who had wronged you. You must pray for forgiveness and re-define your mistakes by taking ownership of them. It is about what you do from this point on with God. When you decide you want to unlock your potential, understanding how the world sees potential is much different than how God sees potential. Your fleshy potential may or may not move you ahead. Your Godly potential will move mountains out of your way while allowing you to be a solid mountain of blessing in someone else's life. Truth- There is still such a thing as disparity when it comes to women in society and the workplace.

Yes, I said it. There is still a double standard. Do not get me wrong, women have come a long way to be equal. Equal to what? Why is it that when men attend a function and act up, it is, ok? Nothing is said about their unprofessional behavior.

I was working for my first large retailer in my early 20s. I was single, not dating, I did not even have a dog. I worked very long hours usually 15-16 hours per day. Yes, Supply Chain-Retail world requires a lot of hours. I arrived at work Monday morning. I get called to the General Manager's office up front. We will call him GM for the sake of the story.

The "general manager" begins to tell me that a few managers saw me out drinking in a local pub over the weekend. He then begins to LECTURE me on how this may look unprofessional, and we expect professionalism while at work and outside of work. I listen quietly. The "general manager' proceeds to ask me, "What do you have to say for yourself"? I was praying he would open this door for me. I said, "I do have something to say. May I speak frankly with you, respectfully?" He replies, "Yes, of course."

I then replied, "First of all, do not ever call me into your off about what I do with my own personal time outside of work. Did these three managers (who I named because HR was taking notes) tell you that two of the three slipped me their numbers and the last one asked if I needed any company later that night?" If you could see his face. The "general manager" said, "No one mentioned that." I replied, "Lastly, these three managers are all married. I am not married or in a relationship with anyone. I can do what I please in my own time. I was not doing anything unethical or immoral. I give you 150% when I am here, and I run the best metrics in the building. What I decided to do in my own time is mine." The "general manager" asked what I was planning to do about the managers? I replied, "I would not file any sexual harassment because we were not at work; we were off the clock." You could hear the sigh of relief. I told the general manager, "You have a problem." He asked what? I told him, "You have a larger issue staring you in the face that you do not realize. The three managers (named them all again) have integrity. They are all married but willing to step out on their wives. You talk of having a professional look at work and away from work, is cheating on their wives very professional? You want these three managers to be role models to our associates and these three managers represent our company." The "general manager" looked dumbfounded. He told me he did not think of that. I told him, "That is your problem. You call me in here because I am a single, young woman who did not take the advances of three managers I work with. But you are worried about me? You do not have expectations for them. But you want to give me expectations. To the core, these three managers (saying their name again) do not care to protect their reputations or their wives' reputation, or the company they serve." I then asked, "Are we done? Am I free to go now?" He said, "Yes and apologized for this happened to me." I told him, "Do not apologize to me. How about you talk to the three managers (saying their names) and have them apologize to their wives. I would recommend you set some new expectations with all your managers about having a good reputation and not putting the company at risk."

I knew the conversation was not what he was expecting. I imagine he thought I would be timid and say I am sorry and cry. Absolutely not.

While at the same company there were women convinced to "fraternize" to get promoted. Many women fell victim to this sham. A couple of women were promoted, and many were not promoted. I was approached several times during my tenure with this company. I did not need a promotion that badly. I had executive leaders, co-workers, general managers, and assistant general managers even threaten me, retaliate against me, lock a driver's lounge, and chase me around a table. When it was the manager's workday, I had to unload the watermelon trucks all day every Friday. I had to order fill loads all day long. What they did not know was that I could do everything in the distribution center. I knew every position. At this time, I ran six miles per day and worked out. I had strength and endurance. Not quite what they expected.

Truth- cute only gets you so far. You can fall prey to this situation, but if you cannot run your metrics, you will not be there exceptionally long, or if leadership finds the next victim. If you know your business and protect your reputation, they will never be able to make you submit.

In the same company, I met many good, honest men who were perfect gentlemen. I had an operations Manager. For the sake of the book, we will call him "OP". OP was a good man. He recently remarried and had custody of his three daughters. We were opening a large building and putting in extensive hours (16 hours per day). I could see the distress in these eyes. I told him, "OP, look you have a new wife and three young daughters. Go home and I will do all your reports and attend the meetings. I will cover the end of the shift. I did tell him I had one request. I want to go tan each night, but I need my full hours. He giggled, but he knew I was serious. He said, "You got it." I told him I wanted it in writing that I had permission to take my full hour and knew I would leave the premises. (What can I say I was young and wanted my tan.) OP asked me why I would do that for him. I told him I noticed the stress and knew he had recently remarried. I explained I was single and all I had to do was work. I am learning the next level and doing the job. This was for my benefit too. OP could not believe I would do this for him, but I was attentive. He tried to get me promoted several times, but no go.

The ones signing off on the promotion was one the men who asked me out. I was passed over several times. I had this high-level person come to me and tell me he would pass my promotion and support me if I went out with him. He told me I did not even need to work and that he would support me. I hope this person knows what you are going to do with your wife. He replied, "She will never know." Needless to say, I did not get promoted. Not to mention, he was not attractive at all.

I sowed my seed in my early 20s. I would not see my reward until much later in my life. I will tell you the story a little later.

The one thing the male peers could not say, "Am I got my promotion on my back." In society today, we are meant to think getting your promotion is ok. You got it. But cute only gets you so far. You know men talk. They will always think you did not earn your promotion. Not only the men, but women will use this against you. **Ladies, we are all human. If you like someone at work and decide to have a relationship, that is your choice. I know plenty of people who find the person they love and marry. It is up to you, but know this double standard still exists.**

The double standard was alive and well. I hurt my career I was brutally honest, and I would not allow the men at work to make a fool of me. I would not fall into their world of double standards. Truth- It is not fair, but it still exists today. I bet right now someone is reading this book and going through the same situation. I did tell human resources. I even told human resources outside the building. I knew our human resources people did not do anything because it continued. I even told the general manager at that time. Oh, it was logged several times. Unfortunately, in the 1990s, women leaders were far and in between. Other women did not stand up for me. Yes, human resources was there but their roles were not defined yet. This does not happen until the early 2000s. The company and general manager had a lot of sway over how things were covered up. I imagine they were scared, too. For all you women in a situation like this. You must know your human resources and federal rights and policies. Know yourself and understand "Mastering your craft". I told myself I would not allow women who work with me to be placed in situations like this. I left the company. Shortly thereafter, the company was in a large lawsuit work women being sexually harassed. It was so rampant that it was a class action lawsuit. I told myself; I would be better than the leadership was to me. Ladies, your reputation is Gold, treat it like the most precious gift. People have bought and bartered countries because of their reputation. I could have been bitter and hated the world. No, instead, I learned from it and ensured going forward, this would not happen with leaders or associates working with me or for me.

God wants to protect you and your reputation. You may feel you have to do this because you need or want to move ahead. You deserve to have it all on the skills and abilities you offer. Do not be afraid to say no. This takes a steadfast course. Do not take the easy way out if you take the uncomplicated way out or cheat on your metrics. You will NEVER be known for your good works. God, see it all. He will move people out of your way, or he will take you away. God will allow it to be you at the right time and the right place.

Chapter 10
"Why Is It Always Her?"

I will tell you another story. I had a co-worker who was a manipulative, deceitful, and extremely jealous person. This heifer right here made me realize this is not the reputation I want in my career. Yes, I said, "heifer". You all know a person like this at your workplace, in your family, or as part of your society circle. We will call her Martha for the book. Ladies, there are many types of women in this world, but we are only going to discuss two for the sake of this book. One is the woman who gets ahead by taking the easy way out or manipulating people. The second is the woman who gets ahead with integrity and ethical acts. Like I said there are many types, but we will only discuss these two. When I encounter this woman, I am in my late thirties to early forties. God knows if I had this same type of person in my younger twenties. I learned from my mistakes and de-fined how I would handle the situation.

I was an assistant director in my past life. I applied for this job, but the company filled the position a week before.

Long story short, I wanted to be in the organization because I could see my path. God was directing me, and I knew it. My relationship with God allowed me to see things that I would have never seen before. I interviewed in July and did not get an offer until October. I did eight or nine interviews. I think they were a little shocked I was a woman who could do everything that was on my resume.

I had to talk to the senior vice president, and I asked him if he was an honest man. He said yes. I accept your offer even though it was a lower-titled position. I was making $20k less at this time. I told him I would fix your building, but when I did, I did not want to be blocked or denied the opportunity because I had not been with the company very long. The senior vice president (SVP) told me they had been trying to fix this building for twenty-two months, and the building had been working overtime for 11 months. I said OK, interesting. He told me no one had been able to fix the building. I told him to let me worry about that. This company picked me up and I had to move to the Carolinas.

I start a new company. I met Martha my first week after leaving a large tech company. I start my first week on a Monday. I have an assistant director who is training me. We go and attend the Monday leadership meeting. For the sake of the book, we will call him James. James and I enter the conference room. He is going to help me get acclimated to my new role. I met "Martha". My first impression was she was attractive and well-dressed, and I thought she would be pleasant. I was wrong. I said, "Good morning." Martha completely ignored me but said hello to James. When we concluded the meeting, I asked James if it was me or if she had blown me off. James told me not to worry about her and that she was not happy with me because I got the job she wanted. Well, how was I supposed to know that? The next morning, the same routine. I say, "Good morning, Martha". Martha looks at me and does "hummm" then rolls her eyes at me. I am perplexed in the moment. I look at James and he chuckles a little bit. After the meeting, I ask James what I do wrong to her. Third morning, same routine. I wait until everyone gets in the conference room. She says good morning to everyone but me. I then say, "Good morning, Martha". She does not say anything. Everyone is looking, waiting to see what happens. In a louder, lower voice, I say Martha, I am talking to you, and I said good morning. The two or three second silence was so thought you could have cut it with a knife. She very intensely says, "Oh, good morning'.

After the meeting, I see Martha headed my way. My guard goes up a little. She comes right in front of me. Martha says, "I wanted your position, and they gave it to you." I replied to Martha, "They did not give me anything, I earned it."

I get into my position and start learning all the functions on the floor. I trained to pick, load, unload, check, office, and merge. Later that week, our interim Director, Tom, came to visit us. Tom comes by my office later in the evening. (I would work the floor all day and then go into my office reading the standard operating procedures). Tom asks politely. Would you like to grab a bite with Martha and me to download your first week? I replied politely, "No, thank you, but thank you for the offer". The real reason I did not want to go was because I did not care to be around Martha. What was interesting is we are working in a large distribution center. The attire is usually business casual, with slacks, a button shirt, or a polo with close-toed shoes. Martha comes in a shirt and heels. She only wore a shirt and heels when Tom came into town. Tom was the most respectful Southern gentleman. I do not know what she was thinking, but Tom would never cross the line. It bothered her when he would ask me to grab lunch with them. I kept saying no thank you because I was busy working.

Week two, Monday morning, Martha tells me she holds the largest record for most cartons shipped in the building. I inquired as to how many cartons that are for the record. Well, my team beats her record in the early part of the week. I go into the leadership meeting and the team is in" awwhhhh." James was being messy. James says, "Oh look Martha, Tati beat your record. I said, thank you, but if Martha had not told me what the record was, I would not have known what number to beat. Later, towards the end of the week, we beat the new record. We have our leadership meeting and James is messy again. James says, "Oh look Martha, Tati beat her own record, and it is only week number two. Martha is clearly up and gets up, storms out of the conference room. I asked James if she was normally this way. James tells me she is a "Ho" and is such a "witch".

I stop and tell him not to ever talk to me about another person like that again. I do not want to hear gossip. James said," It is not gossip. How do you think she got her last two "last names?" He begins to tell me how she had a relationship with an associate and then married him. Shortly after that, she has a relationship with a supervisor and ends up marrying him. I thought it was interesting but insignificant to me. I told James," I do not care if she changes her last name one hundred times do not talk about her to me." He apologized and said he would not do it again. We break record after record. I had to tell the team from now on not to say it was me. It is our team. The team breaks the record. I tell the team I will not stand for any unprofessionalism going forward. The team shattered records to the point my senior vice president called me and said, "I think you put in the wrong numbers. I told him I would double-check, but I am positive it is the number. I then show him two different records of details. He was blown away. Right after he called, my interim Director called and told me I fat-fingered some numbers. He jumped my rear end about reporting correct numbers because they go all the way to corporate. I said, I talked to senior vice president, and I will send you the same reports. I did. He was pleasantly surprised.

I can tell Martha does not care for me. I was on the dock learning to check in freight. She came up to me and asked me if I liked the job. Martha then says, "How long do I plan to stay?" Odd questions. I told her, I am working what does she want? She looks at me with a death stare and says, "Don't get too comfortable." I only say, "I am very comfortable. If you need me to show you anything, please let me know. I got you, girl." I liked Martha, but I could not put my finger on her agenda yet.

The team and I fixed the building in less than six months. We went from being second worst in the network to 1st and 2nd in many metrics.

Fast forward several months. The women in the company went to an event for our female leaders. At this event, I see Martha. We were in a group doing our salutations. I heard Martha bragging that she was going to be the first female assistant director. What she did not know was that two other ladies were promoted, as well. I told Martha that Suzie was promoted. I did not mention myself. Later she finds out I am going to a new state as the assistant director. (She is not thrilled. Tom is the Director for this new adventure in this new state. Remember Tom?)

Martha says to me, "You better be glad I did not know about the posting for the job because you would not have gotten the position. I would have been picked because Tom thinks the world of me." I reply, "You might be right, but apparently God wants me in another state." (At this point, I realize this heifer ain't right.) Yes, I said it. You all know someone like this.) I got to my new state, and we had an amazing team. I loved my time in this sunny state with Tom and the group. A couple of years pass by. The team finds out I am a single mother going through a long, drawn-out divorce, which costs a lot of money. Anyone ever been through a bad divorce or break up? My director, Tom, asks me, "If I can promote you or you go back to Texas as a lateral, which would you pick?" Most people would have said, "I will take the promotion." I asked, "Where would I be promoted?"

He tells me he cannot tell me due to confidentiality. I completely understood. I told him I could not give him an answer and I would rather go back to Texas. My mamma was in Texas, and I was starting to date a young man from Texas. Tom tells me about the increase in pay, bonus, and stocks. I told him until I knew I would rather go to Texas. Later, the company announced some moves within the network. Tom comes back to me and inquires if I can think about one of these buildings where the moves are happening. I told him I did not want to go. He inquires why I would not.

I explained the building with the opening had a director who cheated on his numbers. I knew this because I was the one who found out why his numbers were so good. I explained, "Most people would take the move because it is a title with pay, bonus, and stock increases. I do not look at it this way. I tell him. The company will be watching, and some will want me to succeed, and others will want me to fail. If I come in behind this leader with a "magic pencil" and set the building back to "right" it will drop some numbers until I can build them back up the right way. The company will say, "Look at her; isn't as good as "Mr. Magic Pencil." No sir, not me. I can see through this from a mile away. God had given me eyes to see what the road was down. God put it in my spirited, the ability to discern what would be better. Money and title are not everything. I elected to try to go back to Texas as a lateral. I did not spend money. I had to manage money tightly being a single mom.

One day, Tom calls me to his office. He wanted to talk over a cup of coffee. He says there is "kind of" a running bet at corporate on who will make it out of us three female assistant directors (Shannon, Martha, or me). I tell Tom," Put all your eggs in my basket and not one will break. Let all the other men bet on the other two and they will find themselves losing." Tom wants to know why I thought that. I tell him this, "Shannon is a brilliant woman with an engineering degree from a large manufacturing industry. This is manufacturing (I did manufacture with my work at a large tech company). Manufacturing is very specific and the same each day (boring). This pace of work is not what she is used to, and she does not understand how it changes each day. Lastly, her boss keeps hitting on her, and I don't think she will stay (we will call him Magic Pencil). You will learn more about him later. Second, Martha. Oh Martha, talks a good game and shmoozes everyone into believing she knows what to do. Cute only gets you so far. She bounces from facility to facility so no one sees she does not know but I can see right through her. She is hoping to get promoted because she is cute and uses the 48 Laws of Power. As for me, I have done every position in a building, from the loading, unloading, checking, office, WMS, inventory, HR, buying, procurement, contracts, profiling, slotting, case packing, international, shipping, and transportation, repack, so there is nothing I cannot do. The last thing is I am nice and help people by teaching them to fish not fishing for them. I will change the benchmark for you and everything I touch prospers. Put all your eggs in my basket.

The devil works in mysterious ways. While I am waiting for Texas to come around. I am sitting in my office working. I have our human resource manager come by my office and want a word with me. Larissa in my doorway, looking at me. I look up through my glasses. Larissa says, "I talk to John at distribution center 123 and Martha is upset with you and is crying in his office." I reply, "Ok I will bite; why is she upset and crying?" Larissa says, "She told John you said she was promoted because she slept with associates and leaders." I sit quietly for a second to ponder the information. Larissa says, "Well, anything you want to say?" I said, "Yes, first, do not ever come into my office accusing me of something without asking me about it first. Second, I have never said that about her, but she may want to go ask all the men who have been around her.

Tell John he should not throw pebbles at my glass house. I do not care how many times Martha changes her last name; none of it is my business so long as it does not interfere with my work. It is not here nor there to me. John needs to go ask how Martha got her two last names before going back to her maiden name. Just in case you did not know, one name is from an associate, and the other is from the leader. Tell John I said, he should work on reputation building on how not to sleep with the help." Larissa looked surprised as her mouth flew open. I told her she needed to bring facts because I do not have pebbles; I have rocks. Larissa went and called John. John admitted there were some reputation opportunities with Martha, and they were trying to work on that with her.

We must attend another women's event. We are asked to be facilitators for a new development project for advanced leadership learning. There are five of us, three men and two women. Guess who the women are? You guessed, Martha and me. It is a strategic learning class and a leading change class. We are to learn the material watch the facilitator; and two would get picked to facilitate, and three would be alternates. (Tom is now my vice president). He asks for me to help Martha and be friends. (I tell him I am not the issue; he acknowledged that but asked me to be supportive.) If Tom asked me to run through fire, I would do it for him. Tom was an amazing leader, and I would die for him. We went into the room, and I sat right next to Martha. The first thing out of her mouth is, "I hope you do not get upset." Of course, I know she is going to say something ridiculous. I am a little perplexed at what is about to come out of her mouth. I bite and say, "Why would I get upset?" Martha says," When they pick me to facilitate, and you are an alternate." I come back and say, "Oh, of course not; I will watch your mistakes and learn from them. No issue here if you get picked to facilitate."

The next day we were in the same room. The director for Texas came into the room. He is visiting the facility. When Martha sees him, she jumps up all excited, Hey Ralph!!!!!! Ralph is across the table and says, "Hi Martha'. Martha leans into me and says, "I want you to know I threw my name in the hat for Texas. I know you want Texas too. Martha begins to tell me she knows Ralph and that she is going to get Texas. I told her, good, you can take the night shift, and I will take the day shift. Ralph then sees me. He says, "**Hey girl, what you been up to? Great to see you again**!!!" I asked, "How's the family you been home lately to cut the grass?" Matha turns to me (like whiplash) as says, "Do you know Ralph?" I said, "No not at all, I met him once in 2011."

Day three presents itself. We had a man named Marco stop by the distribution center. Martha and I are sitting at a table. Marco walks by and starts speaking Spanish to me. I reply in Spanish. Martha asked why he was speaking Spanish to you. I asked her how the heck I knew; maybe he was seeing if I could speak Spanish for Texas. I do not know. I walk outside the room for a minute. Marco tells me they are conducting interviews with external candidates first and then will do the internal candidates. When I got back into the room, I told Martha what Marco told me. Martha became visibly upset. In an elevated tone asked, "Why is he telling you? I told her, "How do I know; maybe because he walked by and made conversation?" Martha got up and walked out. (She has a habit of that, and it has not changed over the years.) We are going to dinner; she starts in with I really would like your support. (I think to myself, what 'da heck…. does she want now?" I can hear Tom in my head….be nice and supportive.) I bite again, "What do you want my support on?" Martha says," I am going to be the first female director, and it will be groundbreaking. I will be the first female minority director). At that moment, I thought, "That would be an achievement in a company that has never had a female director in over 100 years in supply chain operations in the biggest node of business (not to mention a minority woman)." I tell Martha, "We do not have very many women in our field; if you make director, you will have 150% of my support." I can tell you I was tired of her trying to pull the "48 Laws of Power" on me. I recognized her tactics from the book.

During my time in the Carolina's, I had a peer that worked a different shift. He must have read the 48 Laws of Power too (only my assumption). My first week, he tells me, " I am here for you, anything you need but know this I am the big dog here and do not "F" with me." I asked him to repeat what he said. I wanted to make sure I heard I correctly. Well, the next day I saw my director, Tom. He noticed I was in deep thoughts. He wanted to know what I was thinking. I told him what happen the evening prior. Tom was furious. I said, "No, I will take care of it." Tom inquired, "What are you going to do?" I told him, I was thinking he was a big junk yard dog on a crappy little dilapidated house with a front porch. The dog is tied the to house with only so much rope. I am the little dog coming to aggravate the big dog. The big dog gets beside itself. Run to tear me to shreds and stupid dog does not realize he is tied to the house. As the big dog leaps off the porch, he gets "snatched" back and is dangling from the porch stuck. Needing help. I told Tom I am about to crush him on metrics. I am going to show him who the big dog really is. I came up with my plan and smoked the goals setting all new records and new benchmarks for the company.

At this facility I needed a motivator to run better productivity. So, I made a "Big Dog" top dog shirt. It said, "That's right I am the big dog on the porch". I gave the first shirt to my peer on the opposite shift. He was furious because he knew I was poking a little fun at him.

Truth, in my opinion- What people do not realize is the "48 Laws of Power or power concepts" only work on people who care about power. It was a number one best seller. I know people who love this book. What is power? Power can only be attained if you allow someone to have power over you. What this book did do for me has allowed me to see the situation I could be presented and how to react. It is like the backstabbing situation; a person can only stab you in the back if you turn your back to them. There is only one with true Power, Amen. I can tell you this book is on some people's top three favorite books of all time. For me, it allowed me to see the situation as it materializes and to handle the situation accordingly. I told Tom how she acted and the things she said.

Guess what? I was a facilitator, and she was an alternate. Yep, you heard me. I decided to handle this position with humility, and I was even selected. As we were leaving to return home, Martha, I and another assistant director were outside. He inquires if I want to go with them to grab a bite or do something? I tell them no I need to go home to do homework. He asks me if it is for my daughter. I said," No it is for me. Tom told me if I wanted to be a vice president, I should go attain my master's degree....so I am working on my graduate degree." I saw her face, and instantly, she was angry and annoyed. I know why. Tom had discussed my future past being a director but not her.

Needless to say, I found out I was awarded Texas. It was time for a new chapter back home. A few days later, I had a fellow assistant director call me and tell me Martha was pissed; she was not happy about the company awarding me the Texas position. Martha was not selected. I called Tom and told him to check on Martha because I heard she was upset. Tom told me, "She is……". I told Tom she should not be mad; I did not do anything to her." Tom told me he talked to her. Tom validated she was really upset. Tom told me she said, "Why is it always her; she gets everything?'

See, my ladies, it was a lengthy story, but I am about to reveal to you how God works.

My trip to Carolina was because my husband, my daughter's father ran us into so much debt in 2011. He took our savings and bought a car lot and did not tell me. I had to find a job to pay off these car loans with some group called "Manheim". During my time in the Carolinas, I ran across Ralph, who took the worst building in the network while I took the second-worst building in the network. Ralph was in another southern state. He wanted to give him leaders development and take them to see other distribution centers. My director at the time told me to get two leaders and take them on a trip which was in 2011. Ralph and I went to Charlotte to a retail food company because he had worked with the president in a past life. When he came to my building in South Carolina, he walked with me, and I had someone mopping under the shipping lanes. The building was organized and very clean. He took one of his leaders and told him," This is what I mean by clean; she has them mopping under the shipping lanes." We got along and talked about how he was from the Houston, Texas area and how I was from the Houston, Texas area. We got along well. The trip was over.

In 2013 or 2014, the company announced Ralph would be the new director in Texas. I sent him an email and it went something like this, "I am happy you got the director position in Texas. It will be nice for you to get back to the family." He replied with one word, TEXAS." I was not sure what that meant, but I was praying it meant I would go back too. I did not know.

God had me encounter Ralph for a one-day trip in 2011. He became a wonderful mentor of mine and one of my biggest advocates. Who would have known this one encounter would bring me back home to my family because I had to leave in shame to get us out debt. I trusted the senior vice president (honest man), the Director, a new director who I loved like a brother when Tom became vice president, and now Ralph who I met one time in 2011.

I became the first female Director in Supply Chain Distribution shortly after I got to Texas with Ralph. He was pulled away to open another building.

See my dear ladies when you belong to God and have a covenant with HIM, **"IT WILL ALWAYS BE YOU....** because God has it for you." No one can stop what God has for you. They can try, but God will put people in your life, and He will take them away so that you can be on the right path. This was a long season, but the harvest was bountiful.

Chapter 11
"Expect Change."

Part of our transformation is expecting change. You will have a million transactions for your transformation. These actions will be incremental changes. No one likes to change because we are creatures of habit. **Truth-** Change is not what you always want, but it will be what you need whether you realize it or not." In the Bible, God mentions on different occasions how silver is refined. If you do not know how silver is worked, I will tell you. Silver coming out of the ground is not pretty or attractive. It is grey and dull. After the silversmith gets the silver from the ground, the person must work and burn off all the impurities. Then it becomes shiny and beautiful. The silversmith continues to work and burn off the impurities until he has a beautiful piece of work. God does this to us and continues to work us until we become what he wills.

I had a forty-year plan, yes mam. I was going to be happy ever after with my daughter's father. He would work with the federal system and get a federal retirement, and he was in the military, and we would have a military retirement. I would work in supply chain retail and handle our money in the present. While I was working in South

Carolina paying off our debt, he had an affair and had a child without telling me. I did not find out for two years. Until my daughter told me about her "baby sister". I was so hurt. I asked him to tell me the truth. When I saw the child, there was no doubt she was his. I had asked him when my daughter was four years old to have another child so she would not be alone when we passed. He told me no and told me he got a vasectomy while I was in the Carolinas because he did not want more children. I was not mad at the young girl. Yes, she was a lot younger than him or me. I am glad she had a child because I never had a second child. Now, I pray my daughter will not be alone. This child loves her older sister and that is a blessing in disguise. It took me forgiving him to get the blessing that is bigger than me. My daughter will have a sister that I hope loves her when he and I pass into the afterlife.

I wanted to get away from debt and then to get away from him for hurting me. What I got was so much more. I had to expect my life to change and be willing to do what God needed me to do. My current company and my last company are amazing. My previous company was amazing, and I loved the company and the people and honestly, they loved me too. I felt like the princess of the company. What I realized is God is my King. I am his daughter washed in the blood of the Savior. I am a princess. I had beautiful and kind women who supported me, and I supported them.

I have so many male advocates that I had never seen in my early twenties and thirties. I was not expecting change with my previous company, but God knew I needed to learn more. I was happy at the level I was at but hoping the company would see me and allow me to take the next step. (Hope is not a plan, but it is what gets you to the plan.) I knew and could see a little further out. I am here at my current company, and I love my team and my CEO. I read a book a long time ago, "God is My CEO by Larry Julian." This current CEO lives this book. When I found out about the CEO and the Executive Leadership Team, I knew it was where I needed to go. My is a senior vice president God-fearing man, and I know I am here to help him, but I am here to learn. I was even told that one of the other vice presidents did not share the enthusiasm that the senior vice president and a couple of the other vice presidents shared. "The vice president (Brandon)said, "Have you ever listened to her talk? She seems slow". Hey, hey, hey. I lived in Texas most of my life; just because I talk so does not mean I am slow. This same vice president (Brandon) asked early in my career why I did not finish my degree. I told him that in the end, we would be the same. You took one path I took another. I cannot turn back the hands of time and get all the valuable skills and knowledge again, but I can go get a piece of paper that says I am smart." And I did.

Later, Brandon became my vice president. I know he did not care for me (at first). I was nervous. It was my responsibility to change his perception of me. It took me two years. I would make him walk with me. Once, on Christmas, I got a double-headed Christmas sweater and made him wear it with me. It was a blast. Little by little I won him over. I was underestimated. I love being underestimated. When Brandon became my vice president I told him, "I will give you 150% and sleepful nights." He chuckled. I told him, "Don't laugh; I am being open and honest with you. I will give you a sleepful night." He looked bewildered. I told him, "You will not worry about this team. I will never have a "jacked" up building. You will never get a call about my building on FIRE. You will have sleepful nights. What is that worth to you?"

Needless to say, I loved working with him. He was great and he let me run my business. He was supportive. Once I called him on TEAMs, his wife was in the room. She pops her head over and says," Tati, I can tell when he is talking to you. He is good mood; his voice is different." I replied, "I appreciate that, I try to you and him sleepful nights."

I took responsibility for my perception. Hard not to like an outstanding performing building that give you absolutely no trouble with amazing employee opinion surveys. I expected to change his mind.

Chapter 12
"Claim Your Purpose"

Claiming your purpose is not easy. Most of us do not even know what our purpose is in life. I was about twenty-eight years old when I asked God what was my purpose that he wanted me to do. I did not have a wonderful singing voice. I sing in the shower and in the car, but it is horrible. I am not a physicist. Purpose comes in different forms. I realized and was shown my purpose was to help the people God sent to me. It was not a glamour or famous purpose, but it was His purpose. I thought I was going to be a teacher, an attorney, or even a lobbyist. Nope, I am a regular person working in the supply chain industry, moving boxes.

I was offered a new role that I got to create a couple of years later. I wrote my own job description and how full range of what I wanted to do, my travel, and projects. My vice president (Brandon) was not happy I took the role, and he told me, "You will never be a vice president if you take this role." It was a little disheartening. What he did not realize was I could see the path. I saw it. (I have a crystal ball of sorts) My warehouse management system

(WMS) manager at the time asked if I was going to take it knowing the circumstances. I told her yes. I will get the knowledge. I might be vice president here, but I have an amazing resume. I already know what will happen, but that is ok. I can see the path, but Brandon cannot see the path.

In this role, one of my first projects was to work with our FDA person and make a "eradication process for rodent control". I talked with our FDA person. I went to present it to the vice presidents and this one vice presidents says, "I don't know why you did this; we already have a pest control process." I said, "No, we have a prevention program. It does not deal with a situation that is extreme when you have infestation that is out of control." This allows us to have a plan if the FDA, or EPA, or Department of Agriculture want to come and

look for ways to find us. We now have a program that meets FDA guidelines. The vice presidents blew it off. Karma…. Here comes the redemption for them blowing it off. About four or five months later I get a call as to where this process is. I told my current senior vice president (Carlos) boss it was on the share drive of the company. I inquired what was going on, and suddenly, they wanted to know where it was. It turns out another large retailer had roof rats in the Mayonnaise, and employees took pictures, and it was not good. I told my senior vice president (Carlos), "So glad I made this process that no one thought was necessary."

I knew that my old vice president (Brandon), who is now the senior vice president over supply chain operations, was not thrilled I took the job. My warehouse management system (WMS) manager (who is brilliant) was shocked at my taking the position, knowing it was a lateral move with no extra money and how horrible the vice presidents in operations were treating me. Most people would have never taken this position if they were told," You will never be a vice president in this role". **Truth**- I told her," I am not subject to what "man" tells me I can and cannot do." What God has for me will not be taken away. I know my previous vice president (Brandon who is now the senior vice president) was telling his vice presidents not to adhere to any projects or suggestions. My current senior (Carlos) was amazing and supported me as much as he could. I loved, loved working for him. I loved myself at this company. Honestly, if I am being honest (Brandon) was using his empowered authority to "retaliate" against me. Brandon could not see I did not want to leave supply chain; I only wanted more knowledge, skills, and abilities for myself to be a better leader. I would have to say, life was magical. I loved working for Carlos. I still love working for Brandon.

Brandon left the company, and we got a new senior vice president, we will call him Frank for the sake of the book. I like Frank, he is good. Frank did not know me but knew of me and my work and how I was held in high regards. Out of the blue and got a call from my current company. I thought my husband did not pay them with a credit card, and they were calling me. Nope, it was a new job opportunity. They want to talk to me about being a vice president. Did you hear me, ladies? I did my interview, and I met with their senior vice president of Supply Chain. I asked if he was an honest person, he said yes. But I could tell he was a God-fearing man. I could see his aurora. I told him if he would make me an offer I could not refuse and my company could not match, he had my word I would come and not take the counter. From the first interview until the offer was seven days. My previous company could not believe it was only seven days (What is seven in the Bible, the number of completion and perfection).

I texted the senior vice president of supply chain for my previous job at the time and asked if he could speak with me. Frank said he could not until the late evening. He then stepped out of his meeting and called me. Frank said, "You never ask me to call you; I knew something was up." I turned in my notice of resignation. Later the executive vice president calls and asks what he needs to do to keep me. I told him nothing, I gave the senior vice president of my new company my word. He wanted to know what company. I told him I could not tell him right away; I was waiting on relocation paperwork and wanted to solidify the final details. He asked if it was a food retailer. I told him no. He asked what I would be doing. I told him I was going to be an officer. The next thing out of his mouth was this," Oh it must be a little company." I said, "No sir, it's not little, just different". This company was a Fortune 90 company. My new company is a Fortune 30 company.

My own executive vice president assumed that only a smaller company would want me. (Here goes the underestimating again). I knew I needed to get the training and exposure of being a vice president to prove to myself I could do the job. It was a training step and development step for me.

We are to have a mid-year budget meeting to discuss the back half of the year. I asked if they wanted me to attend. Of course, they did. When I got there, I sat next to Frank, and we went through details, processes, and finances for the back half of the year. I am fully engaged. At lunch, Frank says, "I know your reputation precedes you, but I thought you might have short timers when you came here." I smiled and said," That is not even my style; you have me 150% until Friday at 6 pm." Frank says, "You cannot leave." I told him I gave my new boss my word. I am gone." They tried to offer me more money and other things. I told them no. I gave my new boss my word. After the meeting, Frank asked me to get a program together to get to 2800 cube per trailer, and we need to get so many million dollars of savings. I only had three days left. What he did not know is that was one of my projects that no one knew about. It was already done. Frank asked if I could do it before I left. I said sure no problem. I got you. Later that week, we met, and I went over the plan. He was a little surprised it was done. Only Carlos ever asked what I was working on. The other vice presidents blew me off. I was sitting on this the whole time. Well, I got Covid from that meeting and had to postpone it until the start date. I had not had COVID-19 for two- and one-half years. I got Covid last week at work at a corporation. Gees. I called Frank and said I needed to extend my last day by two days so I could go to the doctor and get medicine. Frank was so kind and said that was fine. I could tell he was an amazing leader.

This blessing of a new job came from a human resources manager I worked with in supply chain. He did so much extra work and we got along well. I did not know this amazing man called my new senior vice president and told him about me. Who would have ever thought? I had no idea for the longest who gave my new boss my name and information.

Psalms 20: May the LORD answer you in the day of trouble; May the name of the GOD of Jacob defend you; May HE send you help from the sanctuary and strengthen you out of Zion; May HE remember all your offerings and accept them as a burnt sacrifice. Selah May HE (GOD ALMIGHTY) grant you according to your heart's desire and fulfill your purpose. We will rejoice in your salvation, and in the name of God we will set up your banners! May the LORD fulfill all your petitions.

Chapter 13
"Conclusion"

My dear readers, thank you for sharing your time reading this book. We have looked at how you might be portrayed in your day-to-day life. You may be in debt, working to go to school and take care of a home, or attempting to move up the ladder in your workplace. This is not a fancy book, but it is a real-life situation you can relate to. You choose what you want to be and take the environment you have and let it add character to you. We know the struggle is real because we live and breathe it every day, and those six characters make it much worse at times. Be a better role model and do not be one of these characters.

What you will need is to allow yourself to get in the right mindset by having the "G" element, (God) in your life must be fundamentally at your core. With Him you will learn to sow all your good seeds in the right ground so that you achieve your harvest and what your heart desires. It will not be easy, and it will take time. Perseverance and endurance go hand in hand, but it will feel like nothing has happened and you will feel tired, tortured, unappreciated, and devalued at times. Know, you are being refined like silver as each day goes by. But you are so much more in God's eyes. There is a role model; which role model should you be in God's eyes? When you start your transformation, you will find out...." **It Will Always Be You**". You will be protected and blessed more than most. You will have different spiritual gifts at different times when you need them. But understand the devil will come harder for you because you are more blessed and protected. You will have to have a strong mind to know you are always in the hand of God. I call it my crystal ball, but it is real. You will be refined as silver.

When you start to see the blessing come through you will start to expect change that God has for you by claiming your purpose. God sees, hears, and remembers everything anyone has done to you. Every pain, every tear, all the embarrassment, frustration, tiredness, depression moments, and the struggles you have had to endure. He will make "footstools" of your enemies, and your enemies will be confounded and confused. He hears all your prayers. I have listed prayers from Psalms on the resource page. Pray these out loud. These prayers are profound and carry salvation and promise.

Be good to others because you never know where your seed is going to be harvested. I have left resources for you to read or listen to too. I have not been endorsed or paid by any other authors. These are truly wonderful resources that allowed me to Hear from God and handle the daily fight and the battlefield of all the devil tries to do. I want you to know, God is your CEO, your financer, your counselor, your council, your best friend, your advocate, your psychiatrist, you philosopher, and your investment broker. Man (Flesh) cannot be all these things, but God can be all things and bring all blessings.

You may not know how to ask God to come into your heart. You can read this out loud with sincerity in your heart. God will come in. Be completely open and honest with Him.

Remember, pray your prayer out loud and read Psalms for the situation you are currently experiencing. Replace the words of flesh, wicked, man, enemy with the thing or person that troubles you most. Psalms from Solomon and David are still so very spirtually powerful and empowering.

Father, my God (my YHWY, my Yahshua, I Am that I Am) I am here with you because I want to live in your wisdom and your purpose for me. Direct my life and my actions to build prosperity in me to be able to bless the people around me. Through you I will be able to live the life you have desired for me and help the people you send to me. I accept now and believe your Son (Jesus, YHWY, Yoshua) died for me and is the Son of God. He is the father, the son and holy spirit. I know and declare all your gifts and blessings for me to move ahead are recognized now from this moment on. Teach me, protect me, and allow me to recognize each situation so I may work through them in your knowledge for me. I will train and be responsible woman with integrity. With your favor and blessings, I will bless and develop the people around me. I will walk in this transformation you

have for me now and when I cannot walk, I know you will carry me. I will have Faith; you will take me where I need to go even though I cannot see the path in front of me. Father, I thank you for going before me to lay the foundation of my gifts and blessings. I give all glory. In your name, (Jesus, YHWY, Yoshua) it is declared.

    Amen

Resources

Joyce Meyers. **How to Hear From God**, September 2, 2003, Faith Works.

Joyce Myers, **Battlefield of the Mind**, May 2, 2017, Faith Works

Larry Julian, **God is my CEO**, 2nd ED., 2014, Adams Media, Avon Massachusetts.

Taylor Sheridan, Taylor Sheridan, David C. Glasser, Zoe Saldana, Nicole Kidman, Ron Burke, Bob Yari, David Hutkin, Jill Wagner, David Lemanowicz, Geyer Kosinski, Michael Friedman, and Keith Cox, July 23rd, 2023, **Lioness,** MTV Entertainment Studios, 101 Studios, Prime Video.

TD Jakes, **His Lady: Sacared Promises for God's Women**, 1999, Berkley Hardcover.

Robert Greene, **The 48 Laws of Power**, 1998, Viking Press.

My Bible- Spirt Filled Life Bible, New King James Version, , Copyright 1991,Thomas Nelson Publishers, Nashville.

My favorite scriptures over the years to give me strength, hope, favor, and results.

Psalm 13- Trust in Salvation of the Lord

Psalms 17- Prayer of Confidence

Psalms 20-Assurance of God's Saving Work- Fulfill your purpose.

Psalms 27-Excuberant Declaration of Faith- Do not be afraid.

Psalms 26-Divine Scrutiny and Redemption

Psalms 31-Lord as a Fortress in Adversity

Psalms 34-Happiness in Those Who Trust God

Psalms 37-Heritage of the Righteous and Calamity of the Wicked

Psalms 43-Prayer to God in the Time of Trouble

Psalms 54-Prayer for Deliverance from Adversity

Psalms 56-Relief from Tormentors

Psalms 57-Prayer for Safety from Enemies

Psalms 59-Assured Judgement for Wicked Adversaries

Psalms 61- Assurance of God's Eternal Protection

Psalms 62-Calm Resolve to God's Salvation

Psalms 69- Plea for Help there is Trouble.

Psalms 70-Prayer for Relief from Adversaries

Psalms 119- Excellencies of the Word of God

Malachi 3- Refined as Silver

Struggle:(http://av1611.com-kjbp-kjv-dictionary-struggle. AV1611.com)

Tangible gifts: (http://www.quora.com-How-do-you-know-what-gifts)

Element- (Oxford languages.)

Element- Godly -In its primary sense, as denoting the FIRST PRINCIPLE or constituents of things. (http://www. Biblestudytools.com-dictionary-elements)

Covenant: http://bibleproject.com

Principle. (Oxford languages. Online)

Element (http://www. Biblestudytools.com-dictionary-elements) perseverance. http://Marrium webster. www. Marrium-webster.com. dictionary. perseverance. endurance. http://Marrium webster. www. Marrium-webster.com.dictionary. endurance.

Photos by Unknown Author is licensed under CC BY-SA-NC.Online.

www.ingramcontent.com/pod-product-compliance
Lightning Source LLC
Chambersburg PA
CBHW060205050426
42446CB00013B/2994